Volcano Girl

Volcano Girl

A COLLECTION OF POETRY ON
TRAUMA AND HEALING

BY

Sarah Blakely

For anyone who has been labelled a *victim*.

You are a *survivor*.

PREFACE

This collection of poetry was written over the
course of the last decade on my healing journey.
I experienced my first sexual abuse when I was
thirteen years old. Now, at age twenty-six, I can't
even count the times I've been made a victim.
When I was thirteen, I started writing poetry as a
way of coping with the complex emotions I was
feeling. Some turned into songs, but others
remained scribbled on pages in hoarded journals or
typed up in documents on my computer to store for
eternity. I never thought I would be sharing them in
a book someday.
These poems are intense. Many of them are
triggering and may be upsetting. But they are meant
to be that way. The poems in this book were born of
my darkest memories, and deserve to be seen as
they are: traumatic.
That's the point.
These poems are meant to upset you.
They're meant to enrage.
They're meant to burn you up inside.
Go ahead, erupt with me.

- Volcano Girl

TRIGGER WARNING

This book contains content relating to certain topics
that may be triggering to readers.
Please exercise self-care before and after reading

Sexual assault/abuse
(pg. 2 – 58, 63, 70 – 71, 81, 100, 102 – 105,
116, 159 – 160)

Mental illness and suicidal ideations
(pg. 70 – 71, 74, 83 – 87, 90, 93 – 95, 103,
108, 113)

Disordered eating habits
(pg. 87 – 88, 116)

Self-harm
(pg. 70 – 71, 90, 113, 122 – 124)

CONTENTS

The Trauma

Secret Sushi Date

He wanted me to feel comfortable.
So he, 23, took me, 13, out after school
on our secret sushi date.
I felt people's eyes
staring, lips whispering
in this cramped corner of the restaurant,
claustrophobic conversations.

Finally finishing our food
and leaving the tiny establishment,
he drove around town for a half an hour,
looking for a quiet spot to park
where no one would disturb his derangement.
He chose Sydney Street, near my old elementary
          school,
one of my childhood friends lived closeby.

Pins and needles crept up my spine
but I couldn't understand why.
What's wrong with having older friends?
My gut internally screamed at me.
I told him to hold on a minute,
pulled my iPod and headphones out from my
          schoolgirl backpack,
listened to "Remember to Breathe" by Dashboard
          Confessional.

The song soothed my stress,
but I still felt wrong.
(That song never calms me anymore, by the way.)
He asked me if I was afraid.
I said no (I lied), wanting to be a "big girl."
His smirk at my reply should've told me to run,
but I was 13, and didn't know any better.

He dragged his hands all over my chest
still developing, but partially there.
Unzipping his jeans and grabbing my neck,
slapped me a few times, then shoved my head
        down.
I gagged and choked and cried all at once
silently, not to seem immature,
he kept going till he released in my mouth.

I convulsed again at the taste of him,
acidic and bitter and all over my tongue.
Holding my throat, he told me to swallow.
I did as I was told.
But that demon seed took root in me,
became a part of my identity.
My story always starts with him.

White Pickup Truck Ghost

White pickup truck ghost floating down my street.
A strangled breath, smothered backseat.
On the night of a fluorescent full moon,
corruption spreads, I'm not immune.

A stale musty smell in the passenger seat,
familiar textures, experience repeats.
Panic accelerates in my chest.
Stop. Get out. I need rest.

Spit Or Swallow

He told me not to
spit.
I did as he said.
Swallowing
words.

I Am Not Andromeda Because Nobody Saved Me From Cetus

Memories, flooding pools reflecting
tides of my senses refusing to pull
you back to the distant depths of my mind.
I see my hand hit the cold glass window,
staring from my sinking submarine,
the mean mannered moon on that ruthless night,
your sea monster eyes, sadistic saltwater smirk,
and pain, delicious poisoning pain, whimpering
at the hand that feeds me, teethes at me,
screams for silence with speed to my cheek.

The Lead Up To My First Kiss

Memorial Day weekend on a lewd summer night
you came to capture me as midnight befell.
Sneaking out the door to meet you in murky
       shadows,
climbing into your truck with the moldy smell.
Driving through the city of neon and gold lights,
you told me to stay down, worried someone might
       catch us.
I crouched in the front seat without my seatbelt on
while you fondled my face and teased at my trust.
When we arrived at a motel on Alamitos Avenue
you told me to stay in the car, while you rehearsed a
       story to tell if asked.
"You'll pretend you're my niece and your father
       was beating you,
so I'm taking you somewhere safe," you instructed,
       but were never harassed.
You came back with a key to an upstairs room
around the corner from the office, anonymous and
       remote.
Walking into the room behind me, glancing around
to make sure that we weren't exposed.
You closed the door and locked it and I realized
       then that I was trapped
with a man twice my age in a grungy motel room,
       what's a girl to do.

Removing my necklace from behind me, you put it
		down on the bedside table,
then unbuttoned my jeans for me, *so here goes my
		debut.*
Sliding the blue denim off of my childish body, you
		followed up with my shirt,
you looked me up and down as I stood awkwardly
		still.
Striking me in the face, I flinched,
I should've expected this, it's part of your thrill.

You wanted to take a shower with me, so you
		started the water.
I followed you in, you grabbed my chin and asked
		me quietly,
"Has anyone ever kissed you before?"
I shyly shook my head, "no, never."
Translating that as "take it" - you stole my virgin
		lips from me silently.
In the shower of this grungy motel on Alamitos
		Avenue.

Guess it's true,
nobody ever forgets their first kiss.

Lemon Cough Drop

A lemon flavored Ricola cough drop
hid in my cheeks that twenty-fourth night of May.
When you pulled me to the bed on top of you,
it slipped out and landed on your face.
Unfazed, you thought it endearing,
continuing to molest me.

You said citrus would improve the taste,
as you entered my mouth, filled me up.
You didn't seem to mind when I gagged on you,
you held my head and thrusted my throat harder.
Now with every lemon cough drop I put in my
        mouth,
I taste bitter feelings of hatred I harbor.

Ruined

You defiled my first home.
Up the street at midnight still feels like your hand
swatting my cheek.
The full moon sneaking behind the hill doesn't
            comfort me anymore.

You found me at my first job.
Work feels distressing since then, I'm always tense,
afraid you'll appear, like in my nightmares,
seizing my neck.

You took me to my first school.
I learned a lot that day, you became a teacher of
            sorts,
mostly though I learned how to quietly
obey.

You stole my first kiss.
Something special and fragile,
you knew too,
you robbed me without hesitation.

You kidnapped my childhood.
Before you, my girlish mind was untainted,
but you left a mark that distorted it
to a gnarled perversion.

You ruined me.

The Kelpie's Curse

I wandered near the water's edge
to meet a steed, an awful letch,
whose hooves did prove the beast alleged
"Fear not, my child,
care to ride me 'round the stretch?"
He said and smiled.

I let him take me to the shore,
a place I'd never been before,
shifting swiftly and with vigor
became a fiend
covered the scene with awful gore.
Hopeless, I screamed.

He plunged into the water deep
taken with him my soul to keep
into the never-ending sleep
that was my death.
Mother began to cry and weep,
vow'd under breath,

"I'll turn you in, you kelpie sin!
Lock up your vile, repulsive skin!"
She wove a halter she did spin
a cross in stitch.
She had some help to capture him -
a local witch.

The witch called out to me, a ghost,
I barely spoke, a word at most.
They found him down the sunny coast,
arrested him.
Since then it's been ten years almost,
still, I am grim.

Sarah Blakely

The Things I Remember Of You

You'd think I'd recall
tattoos on your abdomen,
examining each inked word,
analyzing the permanent font,
imprinting the images into my mind,
a burning branding iron to the brain.

But that's not where I spent
most of our time together.

I do still remember your taste,
acidic and bitter,
unwanted on my tender tongue.
Your eyes,
icy blue, intensely
piercing through my supple skin.
Your hand,
powerful, loudly
whipping across my childish cheek.
Your voice,
smooth, deeply
growling into my echoing eardrum.
Your grip,
rigidly mean,
constricting around my naive neck.

Yet for the life of me,
the little elaborate letters
tattooed on your chest
escape my memory.

The Maenads

You created a cult of us,
disturbed little girls,
ripened grapes for your wine.

You picked us like fruit,
receiving our bruises,
exchanging worship at your shrine.

You called us away from our homes,
outcasted us in the wilderness,
dressed and undressed us in skins of majestic
       felines.

You entranced us like a hypnotic flame,
alluring though savage,
with soothing words obscuring intentions so malign.

You taught us your wild rituals
up on the mountainside,
tangled us into your sadistic web of vicious vines.

You possessed us like a spirit
through drunken lips
to naked bodies covered in apple moonshine.

You licked up the scent of our fervent fear,
intoxicating invocations
dancing dementedly to your Bacchic melody divine.

Dear Ex Best Friend

Six years since you were first imprisoned.
Are you different now that you're out?
I personally think you should've stayed longer,
but I never spoke up until now.

I never told anyone the ways you touched me
when it was just the two of us in your room,
or the ways that you manipulated me,
blurring my boundaries, sex was assumed.

I never told anyone when we went on that trip
up the grassy mountain range over the sea.
Your wintry silhouette at sunset left a sour taste in
      my mouth,
so I found solace in solitude in the eucalyptus trees.

I never told anyone when you visited me in the
      stygian night,
how you forced me to the ground,
you broke my trust with immoral desire
and the alarm in my head started to sound.

We'd been friends for so long, but only just then
I realized what you had been doing -
you were never a friend at all, in fact,
just using me for the screwing.

Friend // Offender

On the train to visit me,
a friend.
Abdicating his noble title through
savage etiquette.

Hopped the rail without goodbye,
an offender.
Receiving imprisonment after
wicked deeds.

Belated allegations from
crocodile tear flirtations.

Friends don't rape friends.

The Courthouse

We always gathered at the courthouse,
trying to warn me,
that my best friend would be prosecuted
and later on, set free.

We always said goodbye at the courthouse,
walking with him to the bus.
When he was taken to jail I said goodbye there too,
but by then, I was questioning my trust.

Reasons I Can't Stand Hearing His Name

I remember when I first met him,
October of sophomore year.
I remember the feeling of dread he gave me.
I felt sick to my stomach at the sight of him,
dark beady-eyes beneath tinted glasses with
            matching thick black shadowy hair,
even writing this out ties my intestines in knots.
I hid from his presence as much as I could.

(Deep breath.)

I remember the day he made his first move.
Lunch break, we all walked to his house,
while he had everyone distracted playing video
            games in the living room,
he grabbed me by my arm and whispered he had
            something to tell me.
I knew better than to question.
He kissed my neck and marked his claim,
I hid the hickey with makeup in the bathroom once
            back at school.

(Breathe again.)

He pushed me out of my comfort zone, in the worst
      of ways.
He pushed too hard, leaving me bruised and
      bleeding.
He pushed me into a wall a few times.
He'd hit me or kiss me when I disobeyed orders.
always a hit-or-miss with him.
I hated his big fat slimy lips.
Get your spit off of my face.

(Deep breath.)

Visiting home once after college,
enjoying some time alone downtown,
I passed him at the movie theater,
he decided he'd follow me
all the way home.
I lost him around the park by the railroad tracks,
I walked them back shaking.

(Breathe again.)

He showed up at my house at midnight once,
told me he needed to talk to me.
I refused but he wouldn't accept that.
He said he'd tell my parents about all the things I'd
      done.
(meaning what *he* did to *me*)
I believed it though, thought myself a sinner,

or that my parents would somehow blame me.

(Deep breath.)

Walking to talk to him, against my gut feeling,
I knew what to expect.
We sat down at the bench near my house,
I refused to speak to or look at him.
But that made him angry, he grabbed my cheeks in
            his hand,
"Look at me when I'm talking to you, bitch!"
I cried when he crumpled me and climbed on top of
            me.

(Breathe again.)

He called me a slut and said I was his,
while I punched him repeatedly,
I told him to stop,
but my voice hardly whispered.
Eventually he dismounted me,
I seethed, "don't ever come back."
He just laughed as he slithered off into the dark.

(Deep breath.)

Twisted

Pitch dark outside, it's pretty late tonight,
but you're outside my door.
I tell you to leave, leave me alone,
but you've got something to say.
What do you have to say?

You sit me down on the bench and look into my
       eyes.
Yours are completely black,
black and cold, they sense my fear,
but that's what you love to see,
and that's all you want from me.

You're a twisted man,
you don't love me,
with a twisted heart,
just abuse me.

Your hand on my hip, you reach out to kiss,
I just turn away.
But what have I done, now the chase is on,
I can see you smirking
cuz I've always been your target.

Then you said,
"Why do you keep on coming back to me?
I know what you want and I know what you need
Give into the pleasure, give yourself to me
Listen to the voice inside and you'll be free."

You kissed my neck and whispered in my ear,
made me give into my deepest fear.
It's a push and pull that's driving me crazy,
your touch on my skin makes my vision hazy.
It's the way you make my body melt,
the way you say that you're going to hell.

Now you're on top of me, hands in my skirt,
you don't take "no" or "stop" for an answer.
I'm pushing back but you're stronger than me,
finally I get you off and I'm free,
you need to leave now.

You're a twisted man,
you don't love me,
with a twisted heart,
just abuse me.

And I really don't know why I kept coming back to
          you,
you've manipulated me for so long and I'm
          through.
You've haunted my thoughts and made me your toy
but now I'm done and saying goodbye...

Goodbye.

Everyone Knows

"Boys will be boys."
Right?
You're treacherously deceiving,
A demon of sorts,
Not the angel kind.

Remembering your face like picking a scar,
And I shudder recoiling from your lips -
Pressing and shoving into mine,
Enveloping my objections,
Doubting my accuracy.

Manipulative mendacity is your specialty...
Everyone knows now
!

Slander

You look back at rough sex,
I would call it rape, at best.
You always told me twisted truths
how I imagined my abuse.
Is it slander if I remember
you on top of me that December?

Limp

When the relic of my carcass was later explored,
you defended you "didn't know," but I was your
       reward.
Harmful arms gripped me lifeless, hands up my
       shirt,
while awkward eyes watched you spitefully flirt
with my limp body.

My memory of that night is an incomplete puzzle -
some images are full color, some empty or
       muddled.
I recall the call that roused my rescue.
The drive home was hushed, a muttered "thank
       you."
Violation accomplished.

Unpenetrated

My best friend has never been raped.
I'm always damaged goods in comparison
to her perfectly pale unpunctured skin.
Unpenetrated.

She watched me, unconscious,
bobbing up and down, a drunken buoy
in the treacherous tide that was his grip.
She thought I wanted to drown.

Voodoo Doll

Prick me with your nasty needle
as I lay here limp and lifeless,
I've become your suff'ring plaything
though I'm anything but spineless.

Hey D-Bag

Hey D-bag,
I hope you see this.
You know who you are, my latest Insta-creeper.
You know what you've done, you made me a
            cheater.

I have so much to say to you but here's the
            beginning:

You knew I had a boyfriend,
and I just needed a friend...
But wait, were we ever friends?

Define "friend."

*"A person attached to another through feelings of
affection."*

Well, I used to feel affection for you,
but then you went and tainted it,
my first schoolbus crush tastes like rum and coke
            now -
the most obscene liquor.

You never cared for me though,
I was just an easy target.
Damaged and hurting, but you saw that,
you just didn't know what kind of fire you'd be
          starting.

Oh, and while I'm at it...
Do you know how my boyfriend reacted to *your*
          actions?
After I confessed *your* crime to him?
He told me to submit, to do sinful things,
all to prove that *I* loved him.

I guess I didn't love him though,
Because I didn't do those awful things.
But that's his loss, not mine.

Anyway...

This is getting longer than I planned, so I should
          wrap up.
Don't worry, I'll write to you again.

(Look out for #9.)

Sorry Doesn't Change My Narrative

I had a nightmare of you last night.

We were at your old house,
your parents were home.
You took me behind the stairwell,
slipped off my blue party dress,
I told you to stop,
I said they would know,
but that didn't stop you
from pinning me to the wall,
hand over my mouth,
forcing your way into my mind forever.

Sometimes I wonder if you realize
that just because you're sorry,
it doesn't change your role
as the villain in my dreams for eternity.

Academia Suicide Letter

As a young, enthusiastic high school achiever,
I envisioned getting my degree from University
as the obvious next step.
A day away from home and a month into my study,
a stranger determined my chances.
I was 1 in 4 students from my high school class
attending this university.
I was (likely more than) 1 in 4 college freshmen
        women
raped that year.

And while the University has provided support on
        paper;
minimal counseling services I had to pay out of
        pocket for,
an argued agreement to lower my tuition
partially,
and psychiatric care turning me into a scholastic
        bipolar guinea pig,
the bigger effect of my education on my life still
        remains.
I live in a swamp of self-loathing and debt
in the shadow of a mountain in my way.
On the other side of that mountain lies
education, I've been climbing
three years,
lost along the twisted, mismarked path.

My parents fight over my student bills and who will
pay for my therapy and medication
keeping me fighting the endless pointless battle
while my soon-graduating brother may not have an
        education
due to the lack of funds remaining after my
        expensive university IV.
Nobody cares if I'm actually feeling better.
It's being paid for.

So now I'm admitting defeat.
Take my money. Take my degree and erase my
        name.
Suck the last remaining vein of blood
from my arm, and tell me how to make me better
now that I'm no longer in your database.
Now that I'm no longer on your roster.

I am a survivor of a campus sexual assault.

I have no face.
The Dean doesn't know my name.
My story, my name, was kept hidden from the news.
However, my perpetrator got to write a story for the
        paper
on his consequences for taking my dreams away in
        one night.
In his words, he called me his partner,

and I had been engaging in the use of alcohol and
    drugs.
In my police report, a witness's account, and my
    memory,
he tipped back my cups and pinned me down.
But that's not important to the newspaper.
They needed a story.
So instead, I'm painted red. A harlot to "educated"
    readers.

You have no way to prove it but to take my word.
You have no way to prove it unless you're willing
    to accept
my tear-stained tests and sleepless late assignments
as my story goes unspoken without a doctor's note
they won't prescribe me.
But instead you tell me to leave your classroom
because there's no room for anxiety and depression
in these green and yellow duckface walls
of mass-produced college brainwashed graduates.

I'll walk out this door alone
and nobody will remember me come midterms
    week.
I'll be the girl who dropped out.
The girl who gave up.
I'll be another broken body
thrown into your campus graveyard left to
    decompose.

An unfamiliar stone-carved name some passerby
          admires
while walking to class,
no longer existing in campus life,
but you still walk over my bones
on your daily route.

Sarah Blakely

To The Campus Criminal

Save your tears,
I've heard your confession.
I don't care
if you've learned your lesson.
It doesn't matter
if you didn't mean it.
Would you have come forward
if no one had seen it?
You gave in to
regretful passions.
Reckless kisses
turned me to ashes.
But to hell with me,
burn it all down!
Like shots of liquor,
you made me drown.
Now I'm stuck with
intrusive 4 a.m. thoughts.
Sleepwalking desires,
I find myself lost
in this fragile
destination.
To find closure,
I must be patient.
And I can't skip
the hangover you left me with,
you say you had no control,

but that's a fucking lie, a myth.
These stained
glass memories
don't have
a remedy.

Mistake My Ass

I still read your article from time to time.
I still take it out to torture myself.
The same copy I snatched in shock from the news
        stand
on the day it was published years ago,
Monday morning on November 3,
my brother's 17th birthday.

Do you know how retraumatizing it was,
casually walking to class in the morning,
face to face with you again
at every damn newspaper on campus?
No warning, just distressfully there,
following me all day long?

Riling myself into a restless rage,
reading your cowardly words.
I scream angrily in my head,
"What about *me*?"
Not once in this woeful opinion piece
did you mention the effect you had on *my* life.

Not once did you mention that I developed PTSD,
or that I had to take heavy prescriptions to help me
        sleep at night,
or the fact that I was gracious, even kind to you
after the hell you dropped me into.

I went easy on you.
The judge even told me so.

You think you have it bad?
You had to register as a sex offender
because you *are* one.
You had to go to jail
because you're a *criminal*.
You are a *rapist*. Live with it. Own it.

I have so much pent up anger
at you for what you turned my life into,
but also at myself for not pushing for harsher
      punishment.
They didn't ask me if I wanted to write for the
      newspaper.
Even though I was a journalism major,
just like you.

They even dared to protect you in the paper,
while painting me as some drugged up party girl.
Your name was kept secret for your own sake.
We had no connection, no relation,
I wasn't your "partner" in any way, shape, or form.
You told me not to tell your girlfriend.

It's disturbing to me that she married you,
I wonder if you confessed to her your sins,
and if maybe that's why she left you.
It bothers me that to you, I'm a mistake,
one permanent pen smudge on your record.
I'm not a mistake you can fix.

Psychopomp

He didn't invite me to the party,
no,
he stole me to the Underworld.
A psychopomp seizing my soul.

I didn't scream but I tried to fight,
only one witness noticed us that night.
They may have seen my fumbling arms,
flailing in desperate forms.
I passed them the following day
but they turned their sad gaze away.

Winter fell, isolating me in cozy sweaters.
Time ticks and takes forever.
I just want to heal,
the ability to feel again,
But the hell called my body has frozen over.
I swear I'm not giving you the cold shoulder.

Finally came spring,
When all the birds sing,
while the living shuffle about.
They invite me along, they're all going out,
But I shake my head, they don't know I'm dead.
"I'll just stay home instead."

They say "Persephone, Persephone!
Can't you hear?
We've been calling you for weeks.
Don't you want to go out again?
Come on now, join your friends."
But I'm no longer a part of the living world,
Though I have returned, I'm not the same girl.

So-Called Survivor

The hands of Hades held a clutching grip,
caged in the Underworld, wings clipped.
Like Persephone, I've been touched by death,
wearing my blood and screaming to the deaf.
An accepting victim, unwillingly crowned
Queen of the Dead – my own burial ground.

Aphrodite's betrayed me,
misguided favors have left me to grieve.
Artemis disowned me,
indifferent to choice, I'm no longer naive.

The rivers never washed me clean,
Styx filled me with hate and made me mean.
Lethe's waters didn't help me forget,
so I drink from Acheron, river of regret.

The souls of this post-mortem realm cry out:
"Survivor, survivor!"
But still, I hear whispers of the living in doubt,
"Revive her, revive her!"

An August Moon On A Boat

Once upon an August moon,
I spent an afternoon on a boat.
Swimming and drinking out in the lapping lake,
we barbecued at the shore,
it felt so refreshing to swim off solo,
quietly peacefully float -
but when his friend drove me home for the night,
he made it clear he wanted more.

He stopped on the way to drop off the yacht
that he had been towing behind,
put it back in shed but invited me up
"just to see the view."
He cornered me on the deck,
pushing my bathing suit aside,
I tried to fight back with stumbling limbs,
but he had already broken through.

That's why I don't go boating anymore,
I just can't enjoy them the same.

Seduction At The Shoreline

There's a young girl at the shoreline market
selling handmade jewelry,
with all the blessings and favors of Aphrodite,
soaking the sun up beautifully.

He approached her and charmed her so smoothly,
offered a drink and some company
on that hatefully hot humid day at the beach,
glasses went clink but he got hungry.

After talking her ear off at the ritzy bar,
he offered the girl a ride home,
but he had to make just one stop to his house,
which he didn't mention till they were alone.

He invited her into his empty house,
said his wife was out running errands,
it wasn't too long before she realized though
that she'd just stepped into his harem.

He led her through the house to the shower
and helped her to remove her clothes,
she'd been made mistress a few times before
so what comes after, she already knows.

Jailbird

There's a species of predatory bird
that lives out in the wild.
They're dangerous and violent
and leave victims defiled.
One flew in through my door behind me
when I was walking home one night,
he pinned me down with talons
and poisoned me with spite.
He smelled of liquor and cigarettes,
fresh from his prison cage.
I wish I got a better glimpse of him
so I could put him back in chains.

Snake Bite

One more poisonous night,
finishing off strong.
One more deadly snake bite,
a charming gone wrong.
Reptilian arms
wrapping me up,
inflicting such harm
by filling my cup.
Constricted by thoughts,
restricting my breath,
tying me in knots,
reunited with death.

To Appear Coherent Is Not Consent

I remember going out that night.
I remember you picked me up.
I remember seeing that singer play
down the road at the pub.

(3.5 ciders later)

My memory has a blank spot
right after you went in to kiss me.
Next, I remember I'm in your bed,
waking up with your arm around me.

"We had fun, you weren't drunk,"
you said as if it were true.
As if you could teach me how to see
from my own point of view.

To you, it might've been a night of fun
using my body for pleasure,
but what about the after-effects,
the damage you cannot measure?

My First Period After You Raped Me

Retracting inside of me
an attempt to retreat from
the imprint you left on my body.
Squeezing the excess hurt
from this bloody rag
that was my heart.

Get it all out.

Twenty Traumas To Tell

1
One time
I was a child told to obey
I did as I was ordered
even though
he never said please.

2
One time
I was a lured at midnight
by an angler to a beachside motel
feeling my body
become a shell.

3
One time
I was at the pier but
I blacked out when he appeared -
my body remembers the feeling
of pounding pain between my thighs.

4
One time
I was with my best friend
who suddenly wanted me
as something more
or maybe something less.

5
One time
I was off campus at lunch
at a boy's house with some friends
in his bedroom sharing a secret,
frightened, I did as he said.

6
One time
I was at a teenage party
motionless in the dark
being sniffed by a dog of a guy
he marked me as his.

7
One time
I was in and out of consciousness
while he was fumbling
in and out of me
as they watched.

8
One time
I was playing cards with my crush
and his best friend was there too,
the object of my affection didn't object
to letting his friend play with his toys.

9
One time
I was crying to a friend (or foe)
he gave me a drink to distract and dull me
and left a hickey for my boyfriend to find
yet I was called the cheater.

10
One time
I was apologizing to my boyfriend
for my own victimization
and his response was
"do it to prove you love me."

11
One time
I was at my first college party
with an upperclassman acquaintance
he wrote a piece for the paper about me,
a slap on the wrist for the mistake I was.

12
One time
I was cornered at my childhood home
by my high school abuser
he whispered in my ear this would be the last time
as I punched him quietly, it was.

13
One time
I was staying with a friend
and her neighbor found me alone
thrice in a weekend visit
he made my skin crawl underneath him.

14
One time
I was having a movie night at home
with a guy I was interested in
we had to get rid of the couches
when they became too painful to sit on.

15
One time
I was hosting my best friend
in town for a weekend to see me
he tore my bra with threatening strength
and left for prison.

16
One time
I was taken hostage on a boat
after leaving the lake
and everyone else
had gone home.

17
One time
I was in someone's garage
doing lines with the guys
one of them wanted my medicine
the other wanted my body.

18
One time
I was on a fancy date
traditional wine and dine gone bad
he got what he paid for and more
letting me take the bus home in the dark by myself.

19
One time
I was followed home by a criminal
fresh out of jail, fresher from the bar
I screamed in my bed
my roommate told me to be quiet.

20
One time
I was with my boyfriend
and he wanted me
in more tangible ways
than I wanted him.

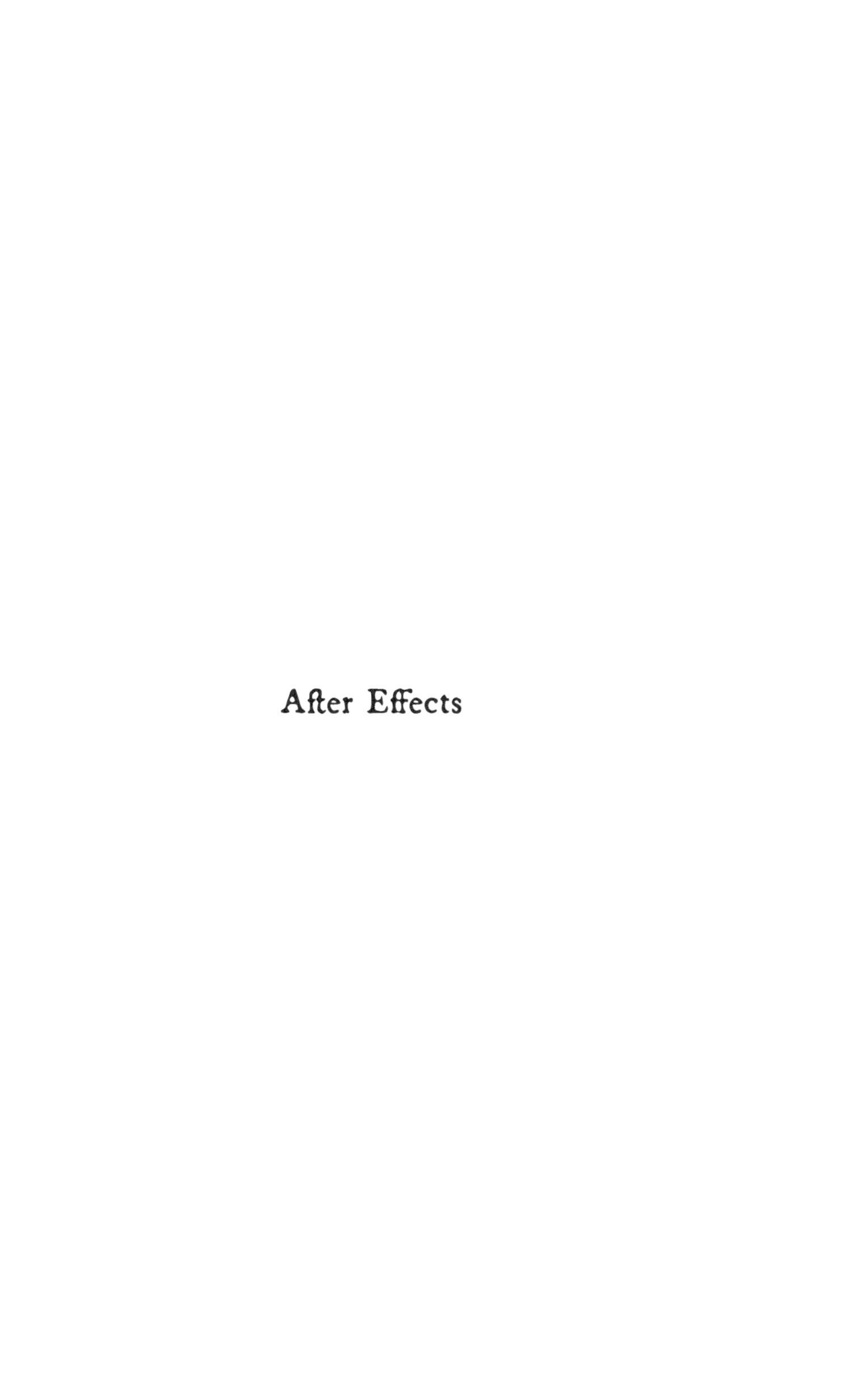

After Effects

Fighting With Phantoms

Delicate docile dreams,
why are you withholding from me?

Grasping my pathetic pillow,
begging for serene sleep,
wishing my broken body were
easier to get up and leave.
Trapped in this prickly prison of
sickly skeleton and scaly skin
constantly captive in this cranium
assuming it's impossible to win.

Hours pass, I lie wide awake,
tossing and turning through the sighs and aches.

Drooping eyes soon give rise
to sacred sleep, long-awaited,
interrupted by nightmares
my brain has created
from fragments of memory
and spectral senses,
fighting with phantoms
in mental trenches.

Nightmare Under A Weighted Blanket

The weight of this blanket over me at night
feels like the gravity of your body crushing mine,
forcing our lips to meet in the darkness, I panic,
my failing flailing limbs have no effect under this
		pressure.
Mouthing the words I've practiced a thousand
		times,
nothing escapes but grunts, a faintly whispered
		"stop!"
before I wake up alone, under a tousled blanket.
And they say these things are supposed to *help*
		anxiety?

Hell Hounds

Shivering in my sleep,
sweating through blankets,
rolling over.
Repeat,
and again,
and *again*.

Relaxation is not where I lay my head.
I rest in terror.
Nightmares like rabid dogs
biting at my ankles as I sprint away,
one after the other, a whole pack
chasing me through the night.

Restless and weary,
waking to the sound of dogs
barking in the distance.
Another horrible hell hound
hunting on the horizon.

Parrots

Intrusive thoughts
like parrots
squawking
at five in the morning
when you haven't slept
all night.

Caffeine And Trauma

Traumatized and tired,
neurons firing spastic,
trying to get higher,
but my energy's going static.

"Feed me more caffeine!"
Crawling to the cafe.
The drug becomes a need
to keep the thoughts at bay.

Each cup is warm and welcoming,
providing quick relief,
but there's a fine line between comforting
and denying these feelings of grief.

Fireworks

Fireworks
triggered flinching,
followed by waterworks.
Fireworks
nervous system overworks
needing pinching.
Fireworks
triggered flinching.

Wanted

I wanted to be a singer
until my voice was stolen.
He wanted power over me,
demanded my dreams be broken.

I realized then what I
wanted
didn't matter.

Not in the bigger scheme of things.

Now I'm left
wanting
a sense of purpose.

Wanted:
a future to believe in.

Volcano Girl

After the trauma,
I went dormant.
I hardly spoke,
I felt
unimportant.
My mom said
I was like a volcano.
She wondered when
I would
explode.

Erupt

I had goals, I had dreams,
but they've disappeared, it seems.
I'm alone, no self-esteem,
all I need is more caffeine
to keep me going.
But where am I going?
It's the same, all this shame,
and it's so hard to explain
why I feel insane
and how life is strange
and it's easier not knowing,
not showing, is it showing?

Cuz I never wanted to give up
and I never wanted to cut.
Now here I am, so corrupt,
and just like you said, someday I'm gonna erupt.
My heart has been collecting dust,
I've been so stuck in this rut,
and I don't want to interrupt,
but just like you said, I think I'm gonna erupt.

I used to say I'd run away,
but I could never disobey.
They say I'm strong, but I break,
I don't feel like I'm okay,
I feel so hollow,
so come say hello.
I just want to escape
but there's no way to negate
my mistakes, I'm afraid,
just kidding, I'm doing great.
But how will they take it?
When they hear that word, that word, that word
(rape.)

When I say I want you near,
but seven years of endless tears
and screams they'll never hear
wishing that I could disappear,
hoping that someone would interfere.
I'm having nightmares again, they're getting more
        severe
and they fill me up with fear.
What a damn nice souvenir,
this gun just above my ear.
This is real pain, and there is some blame
but I've still nothing to gain.
This blood's gonna leave a stain
so I'll wash it off in the rain.
Oh look, here comes the train.

Summer Memories

Memories
haunt the morning
like fog
clinging to the ocean
in the wee hours
before the sun awakens.

Memories
haunt at noontime
like heat,
building,
sticky and inevitable,
a thriving fever in my chest.

Memories
haunt the afternoon
like bees
in rush hour traffic,
buzzing angrily
after a long day at work.

Memories
haunt the evening
like the forewarning
of night
to daytime creatures
anxiously running to sleep.

Haunted Heart

My heart is haunted,
the Queen Mary on
eerie foggy days.

Each gloomy room is
tormented by you,
relentlessly plagued.

I remember the fear
I felt, unimagined
inside this maze.

A spectacular spectre
inhabiting inside
of me, I cannot escape.

Crazy Corpses

Haunted since childhood by phantoms of death,
shadowy spirits and horrible wraiths.
Terrible trauma has claimed what is left,
through all of these years it's hard to have faith.
I do my best but I want to escape
draining depression and manic madness,
every day sane is a day of progress.
If I can balance then I can behave,
otherwise I might as well be possessed,
by crazy corpses from beyond the grave.

Queen Of The Dead

A happy young girl, traumatized young,
only released when spring has sprung.
Made ruler at such a small age,
while seasonally kept in a cage.

Is she a Queen, or rather a captive?
Into this role as a victim, she has adapted.
Though she still holds her power, deep in the earth,
with every flowering, there is growth and rebirth.

She could be called a survivor too,
the myth never says
what she's really been through.

Persecute Persephone

If she hadn't stopped to watch the crocus bloom
would it still have robbed her underground?
Would she still be alone in her cold dark room?
If she never went missing, would she ever be
              found?

Charon's been charging way too much
to be somewhere she doesn't want to be.
These taxes are just too damn high
to be someone she doesn't want to see.

Are you really going to persecute Persephone?
She's only here because of you.
You drag her down then tell her not to bleed;
it's not visually appealing to be abused.

If she hadn't been here to see the colors boom
would it still have turned her skin to grey?
Would she still be chained in a musky tomb?
If she never explored the night, would she ever be
              the prey?

Charon misled her far enough
down this river Styx, she learned to hate.
Cerberus guards the way in and out,
is she dead enough to cross the gate?

Judge her pain.

Cheeks

Well-rounded, lively, youthful cheeks,
bruised on the surface, beaten without a squeak
Soft damaged fruit left to rot and mold
from the inside out, picking away at the old.
Ten years of decay, continually degrading,
anxiety unchecked, constantly reshaping,
the inside of my cheeks must be so maimed,
with holes and ridges, so many bloodstains.
I wonder what it would be like to get lost inside my
        mouth,
in those trenches and caves, no wonder words can't
        find their way out.

Spill It

Holding my breath,
drink in hand,
carefully electing
each word rehearsed in my head,
wary not to spill on my
perfect white dress.

I swallow my past,
a biting liquor
burning in my throat,
struggling to stay down but
managing.
So much mental
managing.

Glancing down at a
spectral splotch on my skirt,
a blemish earned
through a simple
spill of tainted truth.
Never again.

We all have dirty laundry,
and sinister stains that
don't come out.
Shameful secrets
splitting us at the seams.
Bleaching our minds,
erasing,
pretending it never happened.

Wrong Reaction

When you say "cheated"
How I was treated -
That's rape.
I felt defeated
and he proceeded
to rape.
I even pleaded
but he succeeded
in rape.

He raped me and
you
blamed
me.

Black Holes

My heart has collapsed
over and over again,
a series of epic supernovae
giving birth to black holes,
each one an open wound
that gets infected by
everything in my path.

No escape.

I'm At War

My body is a battleground.

Pills like little bombs
parachuting down my throat,
exploding in my stomach,
releasing their secret messages,
misinterpreted by my brain.

Side effects like casualties
accumulating in number,
piling up in the trenches,
discomforting realities of
living the war that is mental illness.

Serotonin

Howling hollow hunger from inside my head,
crying for consolation,
suckling on sweet serotonin to
mollify my melancholy emotions.
But my brain throws a frantic tantrum,
disagreeing with its meal of medicine,
swinging me into a manic attack,
leaving wreckage and torment trailing behind.

Lithium

Side effects include dry mouth and nausea,
wasted, lethargic zombie demeanor.
Tired always, they say "hypersomnia."
Weight gain too, I feel I won't get leaner.

Throbbing headache, heavy eyelids, no end
in sight. Not tonight, ingest silently.
At least there are no mood swings, no pretend,
no mad outbursts, no screaming violently.

Keep me under control, never straying
from instructions of a doctor, always
there to guide me. But what am I paying
for - a service or a lifestyle of haze?

The only drug dealer I go to is
my own friendly neighborhood pharmacist.

Monsters

As a child, I feared the
monsters under my bed,
oblivious to the demons
hiding in my head.

As a teen, I felt the
ghoul inside of me,
unaware of its name,
it wandered free.

As a woman, I know the
beast inside my brain,
I'm aware my disorder
causes me pain.

Weight Of Wellness

I carry my body's weight
along with a few extra pounds -

Weight of past trauma
heavy on my fragile heart.

Weight of my illness
collapsing in my gentle brain.

Weight of stress
eating to soothe ferocious anxiety.

Weight of medication
an uncomfortable side effect.

Weight of others
leaning too deliberately on my origami shoulders.

I carry so much weight
my overburdened muscles mustn't forgive me.

Starving

Starving myself is too easy.

It's too easy to
forget to eat.

It's too easy to
ignore the hunger
as it builds.

It's too easy to
admire my body
when in a state of
lacking.

It's too easy to
abuse myself,
just
because
I can.

Donation

Has my body
always been a
humble donation to the
charity of men?

Am I some
plastic token you
gamble with?
Placing bets
just for fun?

Am I a
tragic trophy
auctioned off to
highest bidder?

All in the name of
philanthropy.

Looking Pretty

Just because I look
pretty,
doesn't mean I don't
fantasize about
plunging a knife
into my chest.

Just because I look
pretty,
doesn't mean I don't
dream of
falling endlessly
to my death.

Just because I look
pretty,
doesn't mean I don't
run my fingers
wistfully reminiscing
over my scars.

Depression is
eating me alive,
and you just say
I
look
pretty.

Makeup

I forgot what it was like
painting my face with colors
transforming me into someone
unrecognizable.

It's comforting not to see me.

Smile

She seems okay.
Maybe she's not.
It's hard to tell.
Look at her face.
"Everything is fine."

Burnout

I've burned through all of my gunpowder spirit,
lacking more energy to give.
Whipping my body, encouraging endurance
only damaging my weak will to live.

I've burned through all of my scrap paper
            affirmations,
filling me up with hope.
Exhaling my thoughts to support sustentation,
is this what it means to cope?

Dried Marigolds

Soon it will be time for funeral games in August,
and then is my birthday in September.
Autumn is speeding nearer so quickly,
while summer leaves a mark too faint to remember.
I feel the departing sunlight waning,
starting to soothe and settle down,
it's almost time to collect our harvest
of the seeds we fed to the ground.
But I didn't sow any ambitions this year,
I didn't even set the smallest of goals.
I'm dead-set on dying in the fall,
you can sprinkle my ashes like dried marigolds.

Sunset

What if
the sunset was
the sky crying out for help?
One final attention-grabbing announcement
in streaks of distressed red and
smears of troubled orange,
nature's grand finale in colors of warning.
One last attempt at connection
before plunging into
night's darkness and torment,
dropping temperatures like dead skin,
cold and lifeless.

Would you pay any notice to mine
if it were even half as beautiful?

Panic Attack Pileup

I remember having a nightmare where you flipped
    the car.
Crushing metal like a can of Coke, sharp edges
    closing in on my skin.
I remember breathing in heavier, adrenaline roaring
    in my veins.
Gasping for air to soothe the confusion, inhaling
    violent oxygen.
I remember screaming in hysteria, afraid we
    wouldn't make it out.
Bloodcurdling and primal through the silent eerie
    night.

This feels like that.

I Wish I Could

I wish I could bury your memory,
a mangled body out in the woods.
I wish I could purge you from my twisted stomach,
throwing you up in the toilet.
I wish I could burn you on a crucifix,
an accused witch during the burning times.
I wish I could erase you from my past,
grey graphite scribbles on pure porcelain paper.
I wish I could escape from you,
a brave sailboat departing from the shore.
I wish I could hate you,
as a venomous vampire hates the shining sun.

I wish I could... I wish I could...

I wish I could see you,
a mesmerizing mirage in the middle of the desert.
I wish I could touch you,
a breeze gently caressing my skin.
I wish I could be with you,
the quiet comfortable presence of companionship.
I wish I could open you up,
a surprise birthday gift from a long-lost friend.
I wish I could keep you,
a domesticated stallion in the stables.
I wish I could love you,
as a human being loves another.

Valley Of Sickness

Every May, the sky rains
fluffs of pollen that cling to my hair,
begging me frantically not to forget
love's scent.

If only it weren't so hard
on my lungs.

Finally fresh air, sticky with a humid forewarning of
       summer.
Shutting the door behind me quickly,
I check for fluff that might've followed me in.

There's no place to go in this valley.
Every alley a memory,
every song a distant ache.
I dream of floating, light as the fluff,
carried away in the wind.
Across the seas with nothing clinging to me,
escaping this lovesick canyon.

All It Takes Is A Name To Ruin A Good Night

Placing aurora puzzle pieces,
buzzing happily with wine and cheeses,
laughter and smiles all around,
a simple slipped name would tear me down.

He hits like a bus out of nowhere,
a sudden chilling draft of icy cold air.
An immediate need to escape takes over,
to avoid this dreadfully sobering ogre.

Trivia Night Flashbacks

I had another flashback last night.

At trivia, out with my friends,
we sat too close to the speakers.
The sound after silences jolted me,
smacking me across the face
just like he used to.
Flinching at the auditory assaults,
cheek whipped to one side,
the sound waves became his hand,
solid as a skipping stone,
aggressive against my liquid skin.
The man on stage,
behind glinting glasses like his,
suddenly looking identical,
becoming inseparable from suffering.
My friends giggled about some actor
who had the same last name as him.
"Bring the Payne!" they laughed.
As if he hadn't already.

Way To Start My Morning Off Obsessively

It's your birthday.

November 13,
my first thought upon waking up.

I wonder if you still live in Chatsworth.
I wonder if you're still an "above average risk."
I wonder if you ever switched to contact lenses.
I wonder if you have any friends your own age.
I wonder if you're shunned when applying for jobs.
I wonder if you use Facebook or any social media.
I wonder if you feel any shame for what you did.
I wonder if you've smiled at all after getting out.
I wonder if you are happy, celebrating today.

I wish I could take that away.

November 13 And I Have Stockholm Syndrome

It's his birthday today.

And here I am surfing Facebook like a deadly rip
            tide,
swimming through the dissociative depths
for a sea star of hope that he exists somewhere
in this vast ocean of digital degenerates.

Do you know how hard it is to find someone
            specific
when somehow every mid-30s white male with
light brown hair and glasses who shares his name
becomes undoubtedly a mirror of him?

Why do I still want him
even if it's the smallest part of me?

If They Only Knew What Happened Here

I can't go to the park anymore
without memories from over ten years ago.
Rusted metal park benches,
cold as December at midnight.
Romanticizing kissing thighs and
alcoholic smiles.

I can't go boating anymore
without memories flooding the hull of my brain.
Luscious lakeside views,
violated and ruined.
Nagging urges to swim far
away from this shore.

I can't go down Leff Street anymore
without memories, concentrated, of him infecting
      my peace.
Graceful community garden flowers,
poisoned and left to die.
Avoiding him like the plague
I'm not yet immune to.

I can't go to the pier anymore
without memories intruding on my body, invisible
        to my mind's eye.
Phantasmal pains penetrating,
piercing and unforgettable.
Startling spectral spirits of
long-gone men possessing me.

I can't go home anymore
without memories slapping me across the face.
Windy winter nights become his hand,
whipping and strong.
Ignoring the full moon's glow
from behind the forsaken hill.

The Blackout

I know something happened,
but no evidence exists,
only intangible echoes
reverberating in my body.
I feel my scalp shrink as he
yanked on my hair.
I feel my shoulder twitch violently from where he
reached out to grab me.
I feel the ghastly breath from behind my ear
whispering he needed to have me.
I feel my throat closing up,
gasping for him to loosen his grip
I feel burning between my thighs and
stabbing pain in my cervix.

Sensations my body refuses to forget.

Imagine This:

A memory comes knocking
at your brain's front door.
But the peep hole is blocked,
and the door is locked.
Your body won't let it back in.
It creeps around in the backyard,
an unidentified man in your mind.

Frozen Memories

Ice thickens like my skin,
toughened and cold,
healing from traumas
too heavy to hold.
Frozen memories
stuck in my brain,
locked in a box
held shut by chains.
Waiting for winter to
thaw my mind,
bring me the spring,
blooming and kind.

PTSD Is An Ice Storm

My first year away at college
a frightening ice storm hit the city.
Classes were cancelled
while campus was frozen over,
pure crystalline silence
hanging in icicles from the trees.

It was the same weekend
my parents decided to visit,
the freeway was frozen stiff
but they made it in around ten that night.
I met them at the restaurant near my dorm,
we ate dinner but I didn't tell them.

How could I casually mention
his bitter deeds back in November,
before the ice layered my heart
into an unbreakable organ,
glaciating my once functional brain with
frigid flashbacks and numbing nightmares.

Rumor Has It

He looked at me, astonished,
like I was some elusive fairytale creature,
disbelief reflected in his face.

I wasn't supposed to be real.
A living breathing fantasy,
an urban legend of a woman.

Offended, I was nothing like his dreamed-up harlot.
Or maybe the rumors were exactly right.

His awkward words echo in my mind eternally,
my name forever a punch line
in this sad joke that is my life.

"Is that you, Sarah Blakely?"

The Terrible New Year's Party

I can't believe he just said that to my face.

I'm sick of this fucking party.
I thought high school ended years ago.
I assumed the drama would die along with it.

I can't believe he just said that to my face.

I'm embarrassed and hurt and just want to leave.
But my best friend is making out with some tool in
      the next room.
His friend keeps following me around like a dog
      trailing a piece of meat on a string.

I can't believe he just said that to my face.

I've become a local legend, a piece of folklore.
A sex icon that professors at the community college
      will study for years to come,
writing thesis papers on my promiscuity and my
      archetypal role as a whore.

10... 9... 8...
When did this become my fate?
7... 6... 5...
Why am I still alive?
4... 3... 2...
What if she always knew?
1...
I'm done.

Happy 2016.

Sticks And Stones

I wonder if you encouraged the rumors,
spoon-feeding my secrets to him without thinking,
without realizing the ridicule he would put me
      through.

I wonder if you found out and dumped him
or if you simply went your separate ways as people
      do,
after all, we were young, and what's that saying
      again?

Sticks and stones may break my bones,
but words...

Words echo loudly like talk radio in my cavernous
      mind,
words weigh heavily like bloody bricks on my
      aching back,
words swirl round in my mouth like vile mouthwash
      for a lifetime.

Up To No Good

"What have you been up to?"
I think for a moment before replying.

Losing my mind to the illness inside?
Check.

Pacing obsessively for several miles?
Check.

Crying hysterically out in the rain?
Check.

Slicing my legs so I don't feel the pain?
Check.

Wounding my spirit with hammer and nails?
Check.

Wondering if my abuser ever got out of jail?
Check.

Collecting dust at my lonely desk?
Check.

Tending my spine damaged in the wreck?
Check.

Collapsing under pressure, the weight of the world?
Check.

Coaxing vaporous memories to unfurl?
Check.

I'm up to no good, as you can see.
Aren't you so envious of me?

Trauma Feels Like

Trauma feels like
forgetting how to sleep
peacefully,
unable to find
comfort.

Trauma feels like
aching in my bones
constantly,
injuries manifesting
hurt.

Trauma feels like
staring out at space
distantly,
intruding malicious
thoughts.

Trauma feels like
bruising of the brain
painfully,
pounding inside the
mind.

Trauma feels like
glancing over my shoulder
anxiously,
awaiting something
evil.

Trauma feels like
sighing of exhaustion
quietly,
chronic cracking
joints.

Trauma feels like
searching for a future
desperately,
looking for a way
out.

Trauma feels like
starving myself
unintentionally,
ignoring growls and
screams.

Trauma feels like
freezing up in fear
suddenly,
crying, yelling, whimpering
"Stop!"

Trauma feels like
unleashing toxic energy
chaotically,
pretending that it's
nothing.

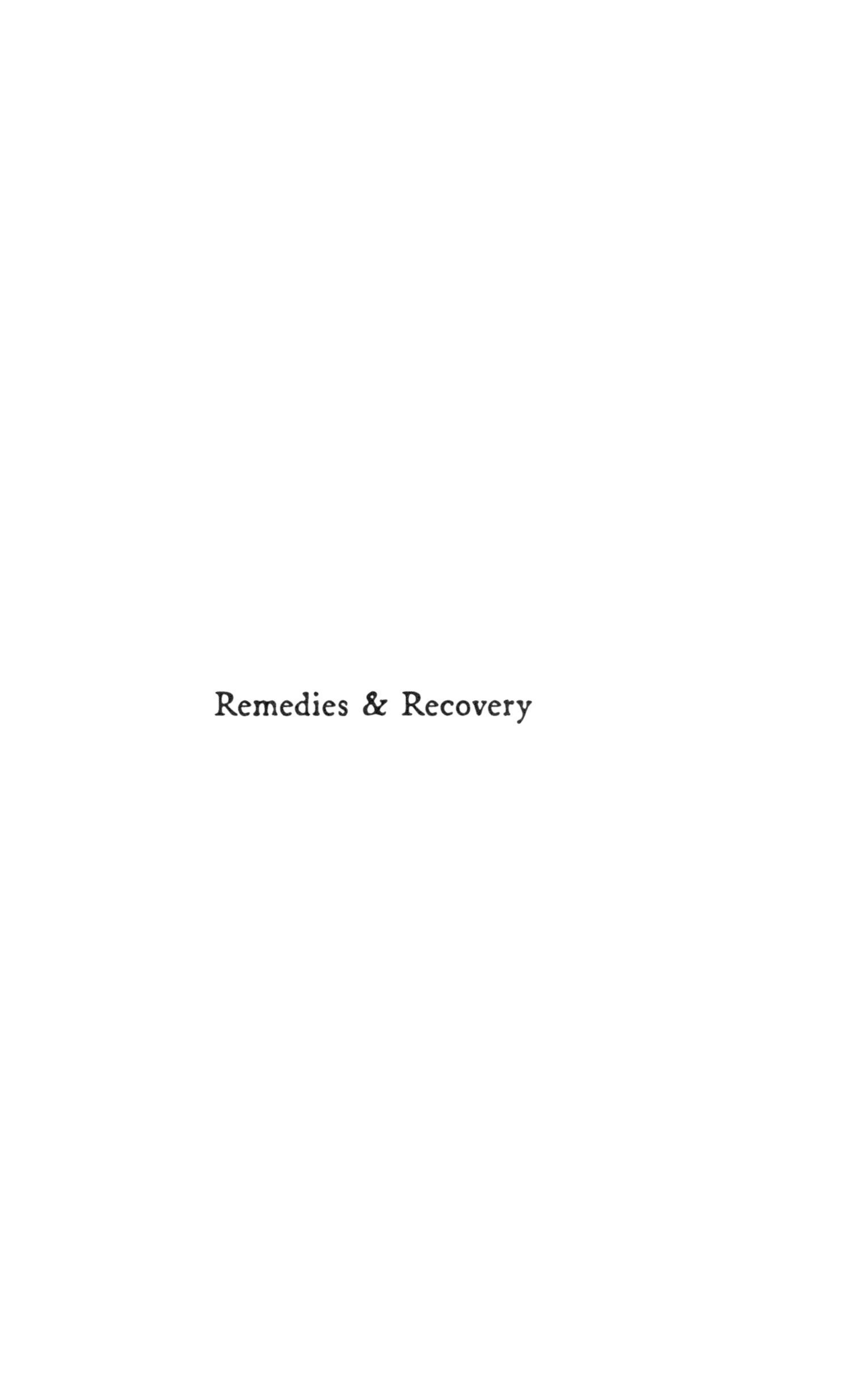

Remedies & Recovery

A Wound So Deep

I thought I was sick,
turns out I'm just maimed.
What I thought was chronic
can possibly be tamed.

But the wound is infected,
prodded by hurts.
Messy and melted,
I still feel it burn.

These scars are so deep,
they've existed for years.
I can't fall asleep
between sadness and fears.

They bleed through my clothes
for all to see.
Now everyone knows
I'm just a pile of debris.

But I'm not contagious,
so why do they run?
There have been a few changes,
for that, I'm shunned?

Nobody likes seeing fresh blood.
Cover it up with cotton,
kill the pain with drugs,
soon it's forgotten.

Scars

I've counted my scars,
invisible incisions,
twenty in total,
ten on each thigh.

Sometimes I still feel
the burning sensation
under my skin
when I need to cry.

After each crushing hurt
I'd slice myself more,
salty tears falling,
cleaning my wound.

But it's been a few years now
since I vowed no more gore,
they've healed up nicely,
maybe I've bloomed?

The Shower

In the shower
I am seen
Imperfect, flawed skin

In the shower
I am clean
Untouched, born again

In the shower
I am judged
Mind echoes, raw jokes

In the shower
I feel loved
Warmth buzzing, heart soaks

Crushing

Infatuation is a double-edged dagger
held in capable hands.
The same strength that
lifts you high in the air,
powerfully pushes you to
crumble underneath.

Call Me

You don't want to call me
broken,
though I'm not exactly
functional.
I always feel like there's a part of me
missing
but you insist on calling me
whole.

You won't call me
pathetic,
nor will you say I'm
hopeless,
but I know that's what you're
thinking
when you don't call me
at all.

Celestial Bodies

Two luminous celestial bodies,
each admiring the other,
staring into nebulous irises
dotted with black hole nuclei,
locked in an interstellar gaze,
beginning to orbit each other,
a binary star ablaze.

Rockhounding

Wading in smooth flowing rivers on
blazing hot summer days,
looking for something significant to
pick up and take on my way.

Staring into the mirror of water,
leaning forward and arching my back,
scanning even the roughest of pebbles to
clean off and throw in my sack.

But you're not a dirty rude pebble,
can't call you a muddy glum rock -
you're a brilliant gem, gleaming and bright,
you must come from the finest stock.

Honeysuckle Sweetness

I think back often
to the day
he found a bee
struggling in the kitchen sink.

He calmly
scooped the insect
onto a butter knife,
bringing her back outside.

He walked
straight to the hedge
of honeysuckles
and with so much care,

and nectar sweetness,
he set the bee
onto a quiet leaf.
He stood by and waited,

peacefully watched
while the bee
collected itself
again.

He gave that bee
heaping handfuls of love,
imagine how he
treats his Queen.

Oleander

I want to trust that you're not
dangerous.
You don't appear to be
until angry.

Comfort seems harmless.
Comfort is home in California,
But I left for a reason -
I hate the heat.

You hate the cold,
couldn't tolerate winter up north.
Freezing ice storms excite me.
You grumble, your hands hurt.

You lull me to sleep.
I wake up and retreat.
You lure me back
with your sweet aroma.

Your smoke is toxic to me,
forcing coughs and sneezes,
suffocating, inhaling
an allergen so appealing.

I've been comatose
two years.
I need to get out.
Moving on.

The Lavender Plant

The lavender plant you gave me this spring
withered and dried, I forgot to say.
It's brown and bare and dead, poor little thing,
though it is pleasing watching it decay.

The lavender plant reminds me of you,
gifting me flowers smelling oh so sweet,
calming my nerves, a comforting perfume,
fragrant wafting blossoms lull me to sleep.

The lavender plant needed love and care
my sunflower soul did as well.
I could've loved both, my heart wasn't there,
I chose to love myself, and said farewell.

The lavender plant is out of flowers,
weeds take over and slowly devour.

Petals

Picking parched petals
off the last flower in my garden,
another hopeful seed my heart planted,
withers in the dusty drought of your love.

Cicada Carcasses

The scorching sky is
stagnant
without the usual dismal droning,
like the empty corner
you left
in my shrinking shell of a body.

You forced me to
transform
into a new adaptation of me,
leaving my old
crackling carcass to decay,
as wings sprouted,
liberated at last.

Home Is A Somber City

My sky goes gray while I recover
in dark and dank cold city gutters.
The smell of soggy cigarettes,
old coins in humid pockets;
like Los Angeles on a sticky, sweaty day
waiting for the metro at noon in a concrete doorway.

I nearly miss the reeking urban,
fragrant with gasoline and rum.
Sweat-soaked cotton and pungent perfume
molding in smoky bars.
The thirty-somethings come
stumbling at promptly eleven-thirty on a Friday
      night,
tossing me their stale coins and moist bills.

Enter stage left, a mystery man, clad in somber
      tones
running from the law, with frenzied eyes,
gleaming, yet warped and
twisted as his curling black locks.
I'm afraid of what goes on
inside that spinning, unsettling,
tequila-soaked mind.

Perched on piers and lifeguard posts
drinking up the ocean till dawn, leaving
empty bottles and ashes aside.
Nodding off on shoulder cushions and
waiting -
for a warmer, sunnier day
in the warmest, sunniest place.

Neon

The flashing colorful lights always
remind me of the city spinning
when we piled in the car with tequila-stained lips
singing along while sinning.

He drove wildly, drunk on tasteless intoxicants,
illuminated by red stop lights.
A seductive beat, his risk captivated me,
turned on by crimson at night.

My eyes glowed green, an "OPEN" sign,
hanging above my door of a mouth,
when his lips met mine, a droning moan,
the sound of neon lights aroused.

Glitter

Suffering from
sequin fever,
you clench your
tight jawline,
deep lines, desirous.

Gold hoops
daintily dangling, I
remove my
long black coat,
revealing a golden
glimmering dress.

Shimmering mirrors,
a private showing
in your dimly lit room.

Give me your
glitter
in my
mouth.

People Can Change

Your eyes are no longer
frenzied, frantically
analyzing.
Your hair is no longer
twisted, chaotically
messy.
Your smile is no longer
devilish, demonically
possessed.
Your mind is no longer
fearsome, warped
madness.

Your eyes have become
understanding, tamely
tender.
Your hair has become
soft, lusciously
curled.
Your smile has become
genuine, joyously
gleaming.
Your mind has become
beautiful, brilliantly
charming.

You are
proof of
people
changing.

Forgiveness

Exhausted
after years of
holding onto feelings of
hostility,
a burdensome backache,
like metal butterflies
clanging in my stomach,
creating an anxious angry racket.

Taking only a simple salve of
honest words and compassion to
mend a wound
you unknowingly inflicted.

Healing
feels like
blissfully tingling limbs,
bodily lightness of a feather,
freely exhaling pent up air,
creating space
within myself.

Forgiveness is
a full-body sensation.

Sunflower

You stand out among the rest
as something better, if not, best.
Of all the flowers in this field,
your sunbeam gaze has the power to heal.
Bright and vibrant, happy smiles,
you make me want to stay a while.
Cheerful cheeks and knowing eyes -
I hope you know that you're the prize.

Friendship Is A Benefic Balm

He is a beneficent
friend.

Marvelous Venusian amor,
jovial Jupiterian humor,
smiles like Solar beams.
Exuding globs of glee,
emitting lilting laughter,
enlivening harmony.

After the storm, the
angelic rays
emerging through clouds and rain.
Tightly squeezing hugs,
warm and cozy, like
"everything will be okay."

You Might Be My Best Friends

The fog glided in the night of the new moon,
icy cold winds whistled beer bottle tunes.
Up atop the mountain, above the mist,
watching shooting stars where we once had kissed.

Rolling the sun roof, as if to prepare,
you remembered I like gusts through my hair.
Standing up in my seat, breathing perfumes,
California oaks with Douglas fir clues.

Driving down back roads, radio blasting,
singing along while happily chatting,
reminiscing on those we've loved and lost,
he was a good man, his heart was so soft.

Before going out I was feeling down
but life is more fun with you two around.

Cameraman

Smile brightly for the cameraman!
Reveal those imperfect pearly whites.
He sees each ugly gaping pore,
spending hours selflessly
glorifying our image,
so that we can fall
in love with
ourselves
again.

The Boy My Mom Wanted Me To Fall For

My mom always wanted us to end up together.
Your name illuminates her face with joy,
like there is still a chance
for me to be happy.

And here we are.
Ten years later.
Together?

Perhaps.

Falling For You Like Leaves Fall For Autumn

His warm skin, like autumn chai tea heating my
        chilly hands,
eyes are roasted chestnuts dotted with molten
        chocolate.
An expertly carved rustic wooden nose arranged
        between walnut
cheekbones wearing sunshine smiles and laughter
        strands.
Affectionate embraces with every gracious
        goodnight,
heartfelt hellos, voice crackling like rustling leaves
        under my feet.
Softened soul as sweet as the perfect pumpkin pie
        treat,
harvesting tender fruits of friendship turned to
        fonder feelings outright.

Cozy coffee shop afternoons in comfortable
        company
turn to midnight adventures filled with shooting star
        excitement.
Serenading simple guitar melodies, harmonizing
        delightfully,
my heart bursts into a bouquet of burgundy petals
        and apricot honey.

Funny how I always seem to fall for him, a
                requirement
in the fall when the leaves are falling subtly.

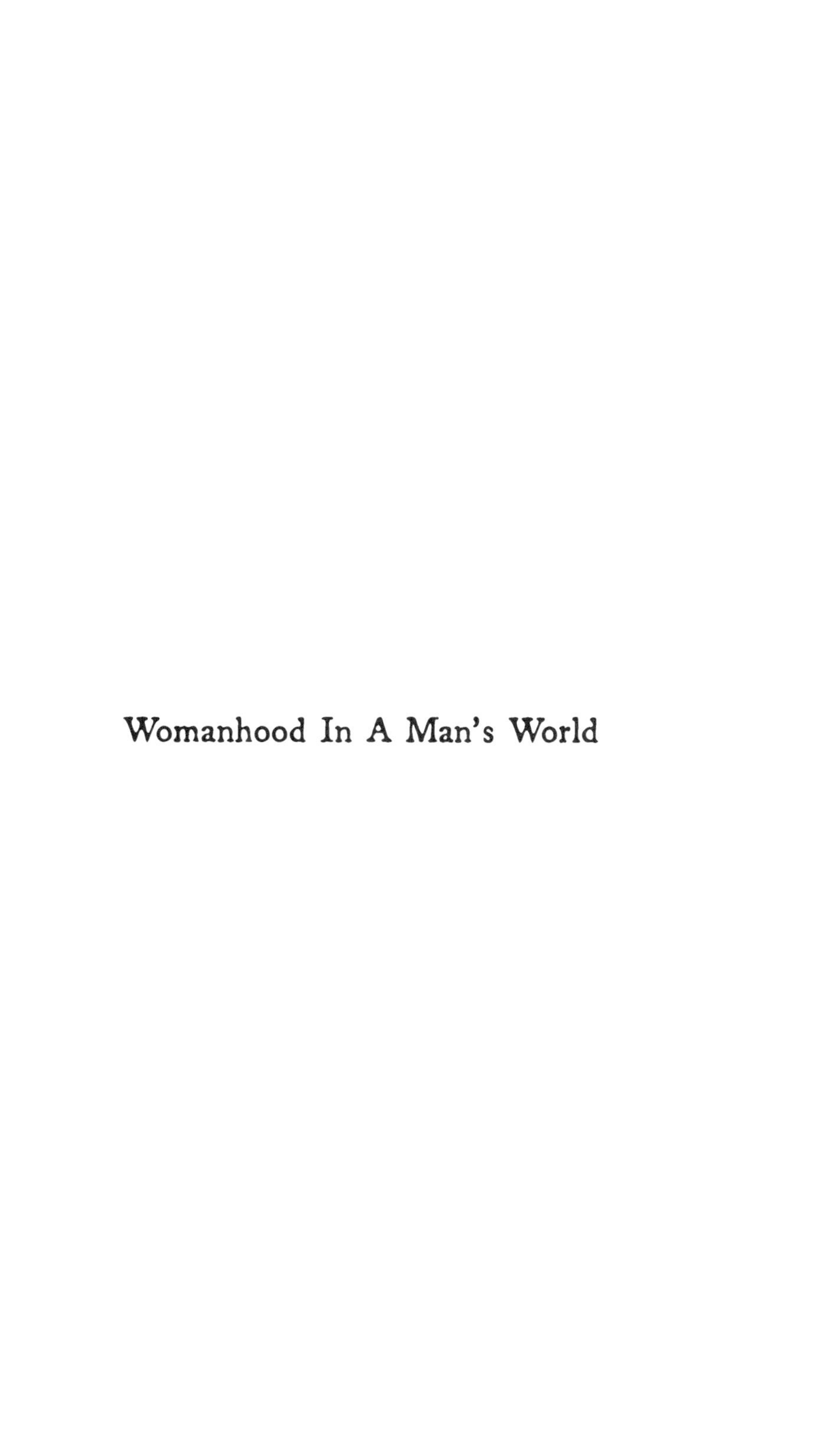

Womanhood In A Man's World

Aphrodite's Love

She smells of sea salt and cypress
wearing rose-colored flirtatious dresses.
She's the beautiful pearl of this woeful world,
emerging from seafoam, hair perfectly curled.

She is within every daughter,
raising all women's hearts to the altar.
We are the golden apple embodiment of
Aphrodite's love.

Solar Power

If you are the sun,
I am your moon -
don't you see a problem with that?

You are the source,
creator of daylight,
patriarchy has grown too convenient.
While my nights remain
a mystery still,
inspiring fear, a feminine demon.

The sun has power,
the moon simply reflects,
I am not a mirror for your pride.
I'm not some orbiting rock,
metallic and cold,
I'm my own star with a fire inside.

Property

Calling "dibs."
Staking your claim.
Marking territory.
Taking aim.

Herding me like a
weakling sheep,
Pretending not to be
prowling like a creep.

I'm not yours to own.

What A Happy Kookaburra

Laughing so proudly
without any sorrow to sing of.
Talking so loudly;
he's never lost anything to love.

Dancing and spreading his wings wide
because he has no reason to hide.
Oh happy little kookaburra,
don't you ever cry?

Singing so softly,
from my cage, watching the world outside.
I know I'm off-key.
Stop asking me why I don't fly.

His world has never been shattered
there is no pain in his laughter,
so I sing my sad canary songs,
drowning out the mindless chatter.

Gold Rush

Remember the gold rush of 2012?
The sequin dress I wore to homecoming?
You said you saw me differently then,
meaning not as some*one*, but as some*thing*.

Before I put that glimmering dress on,
I was just a girl, your buddy.
After that night, Midas had touched me,
you said you wanted my shimmering body.

Persistently prospecting for a piece of me,
I caved, gave you glowing gold.
You hid me away, your secret obsession,
like jewelry you won't wear but will never be sold.

Once you've unearthed every part of me,
no more admired metal left to find,
I already know how this will end,
I'll be the abandoned mine.

The Wind

The wind
pounds
on the window,
an angry ex-lover.

The wind
growls
at the door,
a snarling abuser.

The wind
shoots
up my dress,
a predatory hand.

The wind
kicks
over my flowers,
a rejected affection.

Villains

Protagonist of his own world,
heroic, he can do no wrong.
He's made a few mistakes here and there,
though he never meant any harm.

He's blind to his role in my story,
a lover who bound me in chains,
locked me up in my own body, as prisoner,
a witch to be burned up or hanged.

They always say, "boys will be boys,"
or, "that's how you know that he likes you."
I think most boys are villains however,
leaving too many crying, "Me Too."

Pretty Pachyderm Prey Of Patriarchy

Feminine elephants,
thirst in their trunks,
uncover a cool crowded oasis,
ivory tusks inspiring such lust,
poached by predators
and people alike,
all drinking under
the same ill-fated stars.

Dandelions

We are wounded weeds.

You walk past us every damn day
paying no notice to our persistent pain.
You step on us on your way to work
as we climb through cracks in the dirt.
You throw your misogynist poison to spoil,
toxic masculinity seeps into our soil.
You pick us with coarse vulgar hands,
crushing our sunshine spirit with crude commands.
You yell at us when nobody's around,
and sometimes you beat us down.

Wounded once again,
but still we sprout and stand.

Though nobody listens to
humble hushed dandelions.
You walk right over
crumbling crushed dandelions.

Weekend Pretty

On Fridays
I wear pink but
I don't feel pretty.

On Saturdays
I wear black but
I don't feel sexy.

On Sundays
I wear white but
I don't feel innocent.

I'm not that
weekend kind of
pretty.

Breasts

Flopping, hanging,
draping, dangling,
they serve me no purpose,
designed for a whole other person.

Whether it be my unborn child
or my lover running wild
down the valley in the center of my chest,
these mountains were made for mouths to rest.

Captivating roaming eyes,
sneaking like secret agent spies
down my shirt, peering like I'm dessert,
but I am no easy flirt.

They weigh me down when I'm running away
trying to keep drooling dogs at bay -
with a whistle so ferocious,
the things men do are atrocious.

Jiggle

I can feel the
jiggle
in places that never
jiggled
before.

My feet feel heavier,
my sides feel wider,
my skin feels sweatier,
my clothes feel tighter.

Is it a layer of fatty armor,
protecting me through the winter?
Is it a stressful embodiment,
representing the tired slug in my head?
Is it a side effect
I have to learn to shake off?

Jiggle away.

Bloom

There was no sun the day she bloomed -
only teary-eyed clouds repeating she's doomed,
but she revealed her bright petals anyway,
standing alone, she danced in the rain.

ACKNOWLEDGMENTS

Thanks to all of my friends who have encouraged
my writing over the years, but especially to...

Shawnell, for always believing in my success.

Biz, for inspiring me as a writer, artist, and friend.

Evan and Michael, for bringing light and laughter to
my life.

My family, for always encouraging me to do my
best.

All of my writing professors and teachers, for
teaching me this craft called poetry.

All the men who hurt me, for giving me something
to write about.

ABOUT THE AUTHOR

Sarah Blakely is a poet and songwriter based on the central coast of California. She writes primarily about her own experiences with sexual trauma and relationships as well as struggles with mental health and healing from trauma.